My Picture Dictionary

ENGLISH
FRENCH

Illustrated by Vivienne Bray
Translation by Dominique Cook

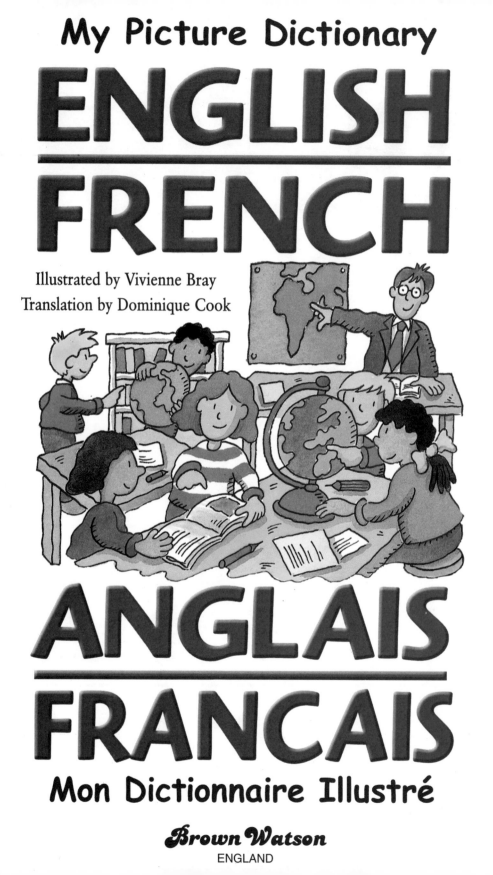

ANGLAIS
FRANCAIS

Mon Dictionnaire Illustré

Brown Watson

ENGLAND

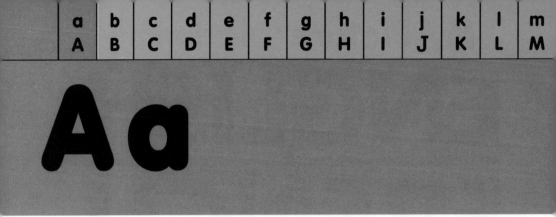

Aa

acrobat / *l'acrobate*

An **acrobat** does jumping and balancing tricks.

*Un **acrobate** fait des sauts et des tours d'équilibre.*

actor / *l'acteur*

An **actor** pretends to be another person in a film or a play.

*Un **acteur** fait semblant d'être une autre personne dans un film ou une pièce de théâtre.*

address / *l'adresse*

The address on a letter says where you live.

*L'**adresse** sur une lettre montre où tu habites.*

aircraft / *l'avion*

An **aircraft** is a machine that flies in the sky.

*Un **avion** est une machine qui vole dans le ciel.*

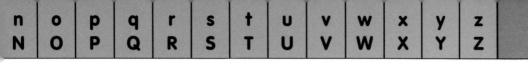

airport / *l'aéroport*

You can see lots of aircraft landing and taking off at an **airport**.

*Tu peux voir beaucoup d'avions atterrir et décoller à l'**aéroport**.*

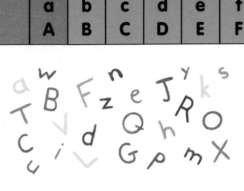

alphabet / *l'alphabet*

All the words that we speak or write are made up of the letters of the **alphabet**.

*Tous les mots que nous disons ou écrivons sont formés avec les lettres de l'**alphabet**.*

ambulance / *l'ambulance*

An **ambulance** takes sick people to hospital.

*Une **ambulance** emmène les gens malades à l'hôpital.*

animal / *l'animal*

Any living thing that can move about and feel is called an **animal.**

*Tout être vivant qui peut bouger et ressentir des choses s'appelle un **animal**.*

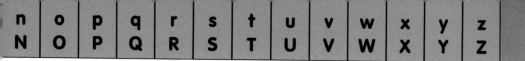

n	o	p	q	r	s	t	u	v	w	x	y	z
N	O	P	Q	R	S	T	U	V	W	X	Y	Z

ankle / *la cheville*
The **ankle** joins the leg to the foot.
*La **cheville** relie la jambe au pied.*

apple / *la pomme*
An **apple** is a fruit. Apples are good to eat.
*La **pomme** est un fruit. Les pommes ont bon goût.*

apron / *le tablier*
When someone is cooking, they wear an **apron** to keep clothes clean.
*Lorsque quelqu'un cuisine, il porte un **tablier** pour ne pas salir ses vêtements.*

arm / *le bras*
Your **arm** is between your shoulder and your hand.
*Ton **bras** se trouve entre ton épaule et ta main.*

arrow / *la flèche*
An **arrow** is fired through the air from a bow.
*On tire une **flèche** en l'air avec un arc.*

artist / *l'artiste*

The person painting the picture
is called an **artist**.

*La personne qui peint le
tableau s'appelle un **artiste**.*

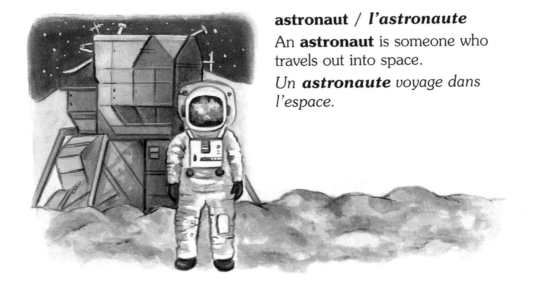

astronaut / *l'astronaute*

An **astronaut** is someone who
travels out into space.

*Un **astronaute** voyage dans
l'espace.*

axe / *la hache*

An **axe** is a sharp tool for cutting
wood. Jack cut down the beanstalk
with an axe.

*Une **hache** est un outil tranchant
pour couper le bois. Jacques a coupé
la tige de haricot avec une **hache**.*

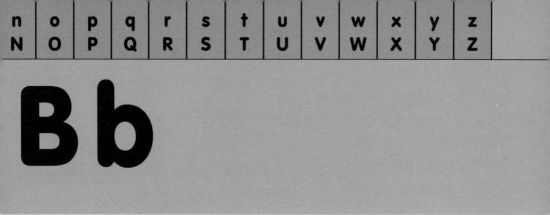

B b

baby / *le bébé*
A **baby** is a very young child.
*Un **bébé** est un très jeune enfant.*

back / *le dos*
The children are standing
back to **back**.
*Les enfants sont **dos** à **dos**.*

badge / *le badge*
The boy has a **badge** on his
jumper.
*Le garçon porte un **badge**
sur son chandail.*

bag / *le sac*
You can carry lots of things in a **bag**.
*Tu peux porter beaucoup de choses
dans un **sac**.*

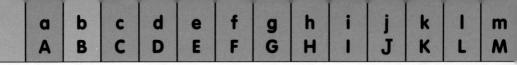

ball / *la balle* / *le ballon*

Some games are played with a **ball**.

On joue à certains jeux avec une **balle** *ou un* **ballon**.

balloon / *le ballon*

We blow a **balloon** full of air at parties.

On gonfle un **ballon** *aux fêtes.*

banana / *la banane*

A **banana** is a fruit. We peel off the yellow skin before we eat a **banana**.

La **banane** *est un fruit. Nous épluchons la peau jaune avant de manger une* **banane**.

band / *la fanfare*

A **band** is a group of people who make music together.

Une **fanfare** *est un groupe de personnes jouant de la musique ensemble.*

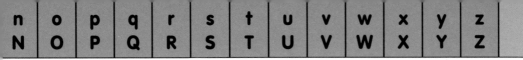

n	o	p	q	r	s	t	u	v	w	x	y	z
N	O	P	Q	R	S	T	U	V	W	X	Y	Z

barn / *la grange*

Farmers keep their cows and hay in a **barn**.

*Les fermiers gardent leurs vaches et leur paille dans une **grange**.*

basket / *le panier*

The man has a large **basket** of flowers.

*L'homme a un grand **panier** de fleurs.*

bat / *la chauve-souris*

This flying animal is a **bat**.

*Cet animal volant est une **chauve-souris**.*

bat / *la batte*

In some games, we hit a ball with a **bat**.

*Dans certains jeux, nous frappons une balle avec une **batte**.*

bath / *la baignoire*

We wash ourselves all over in the **bath**.

*Nous nous lavons de la tête aux pieds dans la **baignoire**.*

beach / *la plage*

The sandy part beside the sea is called the **beach**.

*Le rivage sablonneux près de la mer s'appelle la **plage**.*

bear / *l'ours*

A **bear** is a large, wild animal.

*Un **ours** est un gros animal sauvage.*

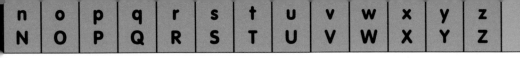

n	o	p	q	r	s	t	u	v	w	x	y	z
N	O	P	Q	R	S	T	U	V	W	X	Y	Z

bed / *le lit*

We lie down in a **bed** when we want to sleep.

*Nous nous allongeons dans un **lit** lorsque nous voulons dormir.*

bee / *l'abeille*

A **bee** is an insect which lives in a hive and makes honey.

*Une **abeille** est un insecte qui habite dans une ruche et fabrique du miel.*

bell / *la cloche*

A **bell** rings when it is time to go to school.

*Une **cloche** sonne lorsqu'il est l'heure d'aller à l'école.*

berry / *la baie*

A **berry** is a juicy fruit.

*Une **baie** est un fruit juteux.*

bicycle / *la bicyclette*

We can ride a **bicycle**.
A **bicycle** has two wheels.

*Nous pouvons rouler à **bicyclette**.*
*Une **bicyclette** a deux roues.*

bird / *l'oiseau*

A **bird** is an animal with wings and feathers. Most **birds** can fly. Here are some **birds**.

*Un **oiseau** est un animal avec des ailes et des plumes. La plupart des **oiseaux** peuvent voler. Voici quelques **oiseaux**.*

black / *le noir*

Black is a very dark colour. The hat is **black**.

*Le **noir** est une couleur très foncée. Le chapeau est **noir**.*

blue / *le bleu*

Blue is a colour. The sky and the balloons are **blue**.

*Le **bleu** est une couleur. Le ciel et les ballons sont **bleus**.*

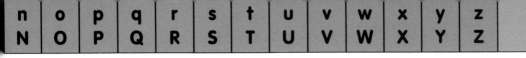

boat / *le bateau*

You travel over water in a **boat**.
The children are in a rowing **boat**.

Tu voyages sur l'eau dans un
bateau. *Les enfants sont dans*
*un **bateau** à rames.*

book / *le livre*

This girl is reading a **book**. This
dictionary is a **book**.

*Cette fille lit un **livre**. Ce*
*dictionnaire est un **livre**.*

boot / *la botte*

A **boot** covers the foot and part of
the leg.

*Une **botte** couvre le pied et une*
partie de la jambe.

bottle / *la bouteille*

A **bottle** holds something wet, like
water or milk.

*Une **bouteille** contient quelque*
chose de liquide, comme de l'eau
ou du lait.

bow / *l'arc*

We use a **bow** for shooting arrows.

*Nous utilisons un **arc** pour tirer des flèches.*

boy / *le garçon*

A male child is a **boy**.

*Un enfant mâle est un **garçon**.*

bridge / *le pont*

We use a **bridge** to cross over a road or a river.

*Nous utilisons un **pont** pour passer au-dessus d'une route ou d'une rivière.*

brown / *le marron*

Brown is a colour. The coat and the Teddy are brown.

*Le **marron** est une couleur. Le manteau et l'ours en peluche sont **marron**.*

brush / *la brosse* / *le pinceau*

We use a **brush** for painting or cleaning. We brush our hair.

*Nous utilisons un **pinceau** pour peindre et une **brosse** pour nettoyer. Nous nous **brossons** les cheveux.*

bulldozer / *le bulldozer*

A **bulldozer** can move piles of earth or rubble.

*Un **bulldozer** peut déplacer de la terre ou des débris.*

bus / *l'autobus*

A **bus** can carry people along the road.

*Un **autobus** peut transporter des gens sur la route.*

butterfly / *le papillon*

A **butterfly** is an insect with four large wings.

*Un **papillon** est un insecte avec quatre grandes ailes.*

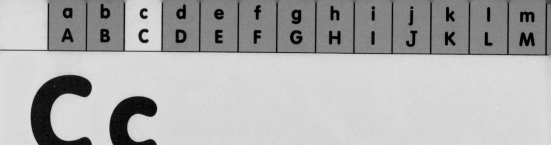

Cc

cage / *la cage*
We keep pet birds or mice in a cage.
*Nous gardons des oiseaux ou des souris de compagnie en **cage**.*

cake / *le gâteau*
A **cake** is sweet and baked in the oven.
*Un **gâteau** est sucré et cuit au four.*

camel / *le chameau*
A **camel** is an animal with one or two humps which lives in the desert.
*Un **chameau** est un animal à une ou deux bosses qui vit dans le désert.*

candle / *la bougie*
A **candle** gives us light.
*Une **bougie** nous donne de la lumière.*

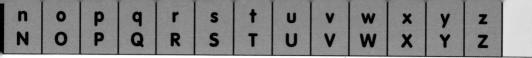

n	o	p	q	r	s	t	u	v	w	x	y	z
N	O	P	Q	R	S	T	U	V	W	X	Y	Z

car / *la voiture*

We travel by **car** along the road.

*Nous voyageons en **voiture** sur la route.*

castle / *le château*

A **castle** is an old building with thick walls and towers.

*Un **château** est un vieux bâtiment avec des murs épais et des tours.*

cat / *le chat*

A **cat** is a furry animal. We keep **cats** as pets.

*Un **chat** est un animal à poils. Les **chats** sont des animaux de compagnie.*

caterpillar / *la chenille*

A **caterpillar** has lots of legs and changes into a moth or a butterfly.

*Une **chenille** a beaucoup de pattes et se transforme en papillon de jour ou de nuit.*

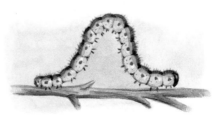

a	b	c	d	e	f	g	h	i	j	k	l	m
A	B	C	D	E	F	G	H	I	J	K	L	M

cherry / *la cerise*

A **cherry** is a small, round, tasty fruit.
Cherries are good to eat.

Une **cerise** *est un petit fruit rond et délicieux.* **Les cerises** *ont bon goût.*

chicken / *le poulet*

A **chicken** is a bird. These baby
chickens are called chicks.

Un **poulet** *est un oiseau. Ces bébés* **poulets** *s'appellent des poussins.*

chimney / *la cheminée*

The smoke from the fire goes up
the **chimney**.

La fumée du feu sort par la **cheminée**.

Christmas / *Noël*

December 25th is **Christmas**, the
birthday of Jesus. We give presents
at **Christmas**.

Le 25 décembre, c'est **Noël**, *l'anniversaire de Jésus. Nous offrons des cadeaux à* **Noël**.

clock / *le réveil*

A **clock** shows us the time.

*Un **réveil** nous indique l'heure.*

clothes / *les vêtements*

All the things we wear are called **clothes**.

*Toutes les choses que nous portons s'appellent des **vêtements**.*

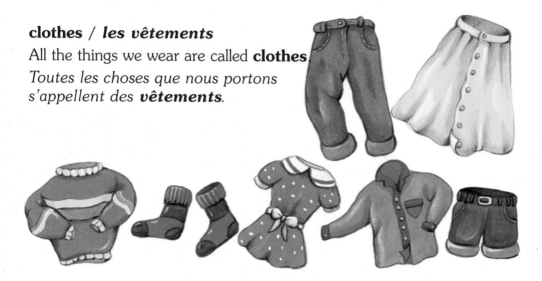

cot / *le lit d'enfant*

A baby sleeps in a little bed called a **cot**.

*Un bébé dort dans un petit lit que l'on appelle un **lit d'enfant**.*

cow / *la vache*

A **cow** is an animal that gives us milk.

*Une **vache** est un animal qui nous donne du lait.*

crab / *le crabe*

A **crab** lives in the sea. **Crabs** can nip you with their claws.

*Un **crabe** vit dans la mer. Les **crabes** peuvent te pincer avec leurs pinces.*

crane / *la grue*

A **crane** is a machine which lifts large, heavy things.

*Une **grue** est une machine qui peut soulever de gros objets lourds.*

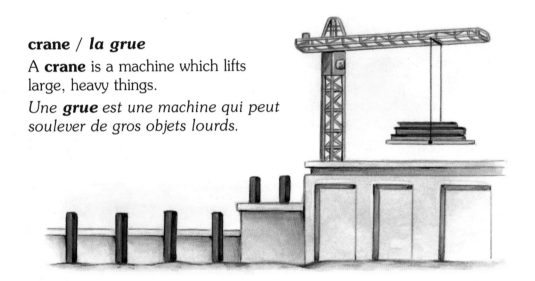

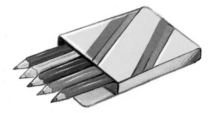

crayon / *le crayon de couleur*

We can use a **crayon** to colour a drawing.

*Nous pouvons utiliser un **crayon de couleur** pour colorier un dessin.*

cup / *la tasse*

We drink something out of a **cup**.

*Nous buvons quelque chose dans une **tasse**.*

Dd

dancer / *le danseur* / *la danseuse*
A **dancer** moves about in time to music.
*Une **danseuse** bouge en suivant la musique.*

deer / *le daim*
Deer are shy, wild animals.
*Les **daims** sont des animaux sauvages timides.*

dentist / *le dentiste*
A **dentist** is someone who helps us to keep our teeth shining and healthy.
*Un **dentiste** est une personne qui nous aide à garder nos dents brillantes et en bonne santé.*

desk / *le bureau*

We can sit at a **desk** when we want to read or write.

Nous pouvons nous asseoir à un **bureau** *lorsque nous voulons lire ou écrire.*

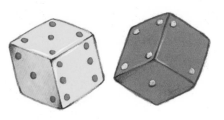

dice / *le dé*

We use a **dice** to play some games. A **dice** has six sides.

Nous utilisons un **dé** *pour jouer à certains jeux. Un* **dé** *a six côtés.*

dinosaur / *le dinosaure*

A **dinosaur** is an animal that lived a long, long time ago. Some **dinosaurs** were big and fierce.

Un **dinosaure** *est un animal qui vivait il y a très, très longtemps. Certains* **dinosaures** *étaient grands et féroces.*

doctor / *le docteur*

When we are sick, a **doctor** will take care of us.

*Lorsque nous sommes malades, un **docteur** s'occupe de nous.*

dog / *le chien*

A **dog** is a friend. Some **dogs** are big, and some are small.

*Le **chien** est un ami. Certains **chiens** sont grands, et d'autres sont petits.*

doll / *la poupée*

A **doll** is a toy that looks like a person.

*Une **poupée** est un jouet qui ressemble à une personne.*

donkey / *l'âne*

A **donkey** is an animal with long ears. **Donkeys** say : "Hee-Haw".

*Un **âne** est un animal à longues oreilles. Les **ânes** font : «hi-han».*

door / *la porte*

A room or a cupboard has a **door**. We can open and close a **door**.

*Une pièce ou une armoire a une **porte**. Nous pouvons ouvrir et fermer une **porte**.*

dragon / *le dragon*

In fairy tales, a **dragon** is a fire-breathing animal with wings.

Dans les contes de fées, un **dragon** *est un animal qui crache le feu et qui a des ailes.*

dress / *la robe*

A girl or a woman will wear a **dress**.

Les filles et les femmes portent des **robes***.*

drum / *le tambour*

We can make music with a **drum** by hitting it with **drum**sticks

Nous pouvons faire de la musique en tapant sur un **tambour** *avec des baguettes.*

duck / *le canard*

A **duck** is a bird that can swim and fly.

Un **canard** *est un oiseau qui peut nager et voler.*

Ee

eagle / l'aigle

An **eagle** is a big bird with strong claws.

*Un **aigle** est un grand oiseau avec de grosses serres.*

ear / l'oreille

On each side of our head, we have an **ear**. We hear with our **ears**.

*De chaque côté de notre tête, nous avons une **oreille**. Nous entendons avec nos **oreilles**.*

eggs / les oeufs

Birds and some other animals lay **eggs**. We can eat some **eggs**.

*Les oiseaux et certains autres animaux pondent des **oeufs**. Nous pouvons manger certains **oeufs**.*

elbow / le coude

Our arms bend in the middle at the **elbow**.

*Nos bras se plient en deux au **coude**.*

a	b	c	d	e	f	g	h	i	j	k	l	m
A	B	C	D	E	F	G	H	I	J	K	L	M

elephant / *l'éléphant*

An **elephant** is a large, grey animal with big ears, and a very long nose, called a trunk.

*Un **éléphant** est un gros animal gris avec de grandes oreilles et un très long nez, que l'on appelle une trompe.*

empty / *vide*

The box is **empty**. There is nothing in the box.

*La boîte est **vide**. Il n'y a rien dans la boîte.*

end / *le bout*

The **end** is the last of something. Each dog has an **end** of the rope.

*Le **bout** est la fin de quelque chose. Chaque chien tient un **bout** de la corde.*

envelope / *l'enveloppe*

When we have written a letter, we put it into an **envelope** before we post it.

*Lorsque nous avons écrit une lettre, nous la mettons dans une **enveloppe** avant de la poster.*

Eskimo / l'Eskimo

An **Eskimo** lives in a very cold part of the world. **Eskimos** have to wear warm, furry clothes.

*Un **Eskimo** habite dans un endroit très froid du monde. Les **Eskimos** portent des vêtements chauds en fourrure.*

exercises / *les exercices*

The children are doing **exercises**. **Exercises** are special movements to keep our bodies fit.

*Les enfants font des **exercices**. Les **exercices** sont des mouvements spéciaux pour maintenir nos corps en forme.*

eye / *l'oeil*

The **eye** is the part of our body through which we see. We have two **eyes**.

*L'**oeil** est la partie du corps par laquelle nous voyons. Nous avons deux **yeux**.*

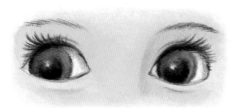

F f

face / *le visage*

The **face** is on the front of the head.
*Le **visage** se trouve sur le devant de la tête.*

fair / *la foire*

We can have lots of fun at a **fair**.
*Nous pouvons bien nous amuser à la **foire**.*

farm / *la ferme*

On a **farm**, food is grown and **farm** animals are kept.
*A la **ferme**, on fait pousser de la nourriture et on élève des animaux de **ferme**.*

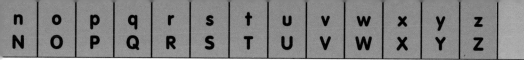

n	o	p	q	r	s	t	u	v	w	x	y	z
N	O	P	Q	R	S	T	U	V	W	X	Y	Z

feather / *la plume*

A **feather** is very light. **Feathers** grow on birds.

*Une **plume** est très légère. Les **plumes** poussent sur les oiseaux.*

fence / *la clôture*

You put a **fence** of wood or wire round your garden.

*Tu mets une **clôture** en bois ou en fil de fer autour de ton jardin.*

finger / *le doigt*

A **finger** is a part of the hand. We have eight **fingers** and two thumbs.

*Un **doigt** fait partie de la main. Nous avons huit **doigts** et deux pouces.*

fire / *le feu*

When something is burning, there is a **fire**. A **fire** is very hot.

*Lorsque quelque chose brûle, il y a un **feu**. Un **feu** est très chaud.*

fish / *poisson*

A **fish** is an animal that lives in the water.

*Un **poisson** est un animal qui vit dans l'eau.*

flag / *le drapeau*

A **flag** is a coloured piece of cloth or paper. This is the pirates' **flag**.

*Un **drapeau** est un morceau de tissu ou de papier en couleur. Voici le **drapeau** des pirates.*

flowers / *les fleurs*

Flowers are pretty and they smell nice. A **flower** is the part of a plant with seeds in it.

*Les **fleurs** sont jolies et elles sentent bon. La **fleur** est la partie d'une plante qui contient des graines.*

food / *la nourriture*

Food is what we eat. Everything needs **food** to stay alive.

*La **nourriture** est ce que nous mangeons. Tout a besoin de **nourriture** pour rester en vie.*

foot / *le pied*

At the end of each leg, we have a **foot.** We stand on our **feet.**

*Au bout de chaque jambe, nous avons un **pied**. Nous nous tenons debout sur nos **pieds**.*

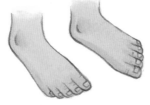

forest / *la forêt*

There are lots of trees in a **forest.**

*Il y a beaucoup d'arbres dans une **forêt**.*

fountain / *la fontaine*

A **fountain** shoots water up into the air.

*Une **fontaine** lance de l'eau en l'air.*

fox / *le renard*

A **fox** is a kind of wild dog, with a bushy tail.

Un **renard** est un genre de chien sauvage, avec une queue touffue.

frog / *la grenouille*

A **frog** is a small animal that lives near water. **Frogs** jump and have webbed feet.

*Une **grenouille** est un petit animal qui vit près de l'eau. Les **grenouilles** sautent et ont des pattes palmées.*

fruit / *le fruit*

Some plants have **fruit**. We eat **fruit**, like oranges, bananas and strawberries.

*Certaines plantes ont des **fruits**. Nous mangeons des **fruits**, comme les oranges, les bananes et les fraises.*

full / *plein*

When you cannot get any more into something, it is **full**.

*Lorsque tu ne peux plus rien mettre dans quelque chose, c'est **plein**.*

funny / *amusant*

The clown makes the children laugh. They think the clown is **funny**.

*Le clown fait rire les enfants. Ils trouvent que le clown est **amusant**.*

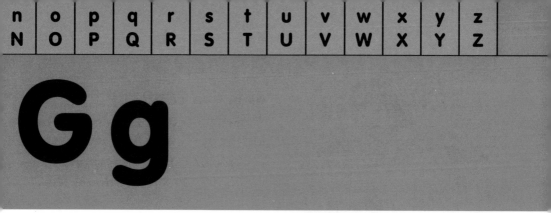

G g

garage / *le garage*

The car is in the **garage**.

*La voiture est dans le **garage**.*

garden / *le jardin*

We grow grass and flowers in a **garden**. We can play in the **garden**.

*Nous faisons pousser de l'herbe et des fleurs dans un **jardin**. Nous pouvons jouer dans le **jardin**.*

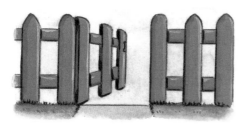

gate / *la grille*

A **gate** is like a door in a fence.

*Une **grille** est comme une porte dans une clôture.*

giant / *le géant*

A **giant** is a very big person in a fairy tale.

*Un **géant** est une très grande personne dans un conte de fées.*

giraffe / *la girafe*

A **giraffe** is a wild animal with long legs and a very long neck.

*Une **girafe** est un animal sauvage avec de longues jambes et un très long cou.*

girl / *la fille*

A female child is a **girl**.

*Un enfant femelle est une **fille**.*

gloves / *les gants*

We wear **gloves** to keep our hands warm.

*Nous portons des **gants** pour avoir chaud aux mains.*

goat / *la chèvre*

A **goat** is like a large sheep with horns and a beard.

*Une **chèvre** ressemble à un gros mouton avec des cornes et une barbe.*

goldfish / *le poisson rouge*

We keep **goldfish** as pets in a tank.

*Nous mettons des **poissons rouges** de compagnie dans un aquarium.*

grass / *l'herbe*

Grass is green, and grows almost everywhere. We have to cut the **grass** in the garden.

*L'**herbe** est verte et pousse presque partout. Nous devons couper l'**herbe** du jardin.*

green / *le vert*

Green is a colour. The jumper is **green**. So is the scarf.

*Le **vert** est une couleur. Le chandail est **vert**. L'écharpe aussi.*

grey / *le gris*

Grey is a colour. Clouds are **grey** when it is raining.

*Le **gris** est une couleur. Les nuages sont **gris** quand il pleut.*

Hh

hammer / *le marteau*

A **hammer** is a tool for banging in nails.

*Un **marteau** est un outil pour enfoncer les clous.*

hamster / *le hamster*

A **hamster** is a small, furry animal. **Hamsters** keep food in their cheeks.

*Un **hamster** est un petit animal à poils. Les **hamsters** gardent leur nourriture dans leurs joues.*

hand / *la main*

We have a **hand** at the end of each arm. Our **hands** are for holding and touching things.

*Nous avons une **main** au bout de chaque bras. Nos **mains** nous servent à tenir et à toucher les choses.*

handkerchief / *le mouchoir*

We use a **handkerchief** to wipe our nose when we have a cold.

*Nous utilisons un **mouchoir** pour nous moucher quand nous avons un rhume.*

harp / *la harpe*

We pluck the strings on a **harp** to make music.

Nous pinçons les cordes d'une **harpe** *pour jouer de la musique.*

hat / *le chapeau*

We wear a **hat** on our head. This is a man's **hat**.

Nous portons un **chapeau** *sur la tête. Voici un* **chapeau** *d'homme.*

hay / *la paille*

Hay is dried grass and is used for feeding cows and sheep.

La **paille** *est de l'herbe séchée qui sert à nourrir les vaches et les moutons.*

head / *la tête*

Our **head** is on our shoulders. The face is the front of the **head**.

Notre **tête** *se trouve sur nos épaules. Le visage est le devant de la* **tête**.

hedge / *la haie*

A **hedge** is a row of bushes which makes a fence round a field.

Une **haie** *est une ligne de buissons qui forme une clôture autour d'un champ.*

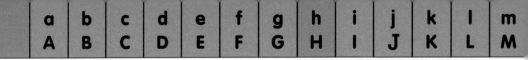

heel / *le talon*

The **heel** is the back part of the foot.
*Le **talon** est la partie arrière du pied.*

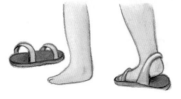

helicopter / *l'hélicoptère*

A **helicopter** is an aircraft without wings which can fly straight up into the air.
*Un **hélicoptère** est un avion sans ailes qui peut s'élever tout droit dans l'air.*

helmet / *le casque*

A **helmet** is a strong cover for the head. We wear a **helmet** to keep our head safe.
*Un **casque** est une protection solide pour la tête. Nous portons un **casque** pour protéger notre tête.*

hen / *la poule*

A female bird is called a **hen**. We can eat the eggs of farmyard **hens**.
*La femelle d'un oiseau s'appelle une **poule**. Nous pouvons manger les oeufs des **poules** de la ferme.*

hill / *la colline*

A **hill** is higher than the land around it. **Hills** are not as high as mountains.
*Une **colline** est plus élevée que le terrain autour. Les **collines** ne sont pas aussi élevées que les montagnes.*

hook / *le portemanteau*

We can hang a coat on a **hook**.

*Nous pouvons accrocher un manteau à un **portemanteau**.*

---

horn / *la corne* / *le bois*

Horns are the pointed bits on the heads of deer. A rhino has a **horn** on its nose.

*Les **bois** sont les morceaux pointus sur la tête des cerfs. Un rhinocéros a une **corne** sur son museau.*

horse / *le cheval*

A **horse** is an animal which is used for riding, or for pulling carts.

*Un **cheval** est un animal que l'on monte ou qui tire des chariots.*

---

hospital / *l'hôpital*

When we are very sick, we have to go to **hospital**.

*Lorsque nous sommes très malades, nous devons aller à **l'hôpital**.*

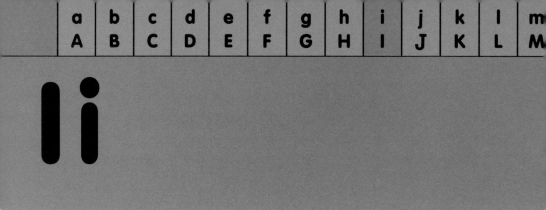

Ii

iceberg / *l'iceberg*

A very large block of ice which floats in the sea is an **iceberg**.

*Un très gros morceau de glace qui flotte dans la mer s'appelle un **iceberg**.*

ice cream / *la crème glacée*

Ice cream is cold and sweet. Eating **ice cream** is great.

*La **crème glacée** est froide et sucrée. Manger de la **crème glacée** est agréable.*

icicles / *les stalactites*

Icicles are pointed spikes of frozen water.

*Les **stalactites** sont des aiguilles d'eau gelée.*

icing / *le glaçage*

Icing is the sweet topping put on birthday cakes.

*Le **glaçage** est la garniture sucrée des gâteaux d'anniversaire.*

igloo / *l'igloo*

Eskimos live in houses called **igloos**, made from frozen snow.

*Les Eskimos habitent des maisons que l'on appelle des **igloos**, construits avec de la neige gelée.*

insects / *les insectes*

Insects are small animals with six legs. Some **insects** are small, some are big.

*Les **insectes** sont de petits animaux à six pattes. Certains **insectes** sont petits, d'autres sont gros.*

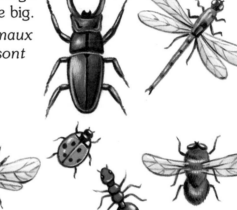

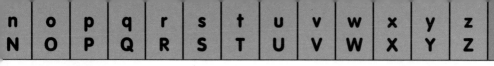

iron / *le fer à repasser*

We press clothes with an **iron**.

*Nous repassons les vêtements avec un **fer à repasser**.*

island / *l'île*

An **island** is a piece of land with water all around it.

*Une **île** est un morceau de terre entouré d'eau.*

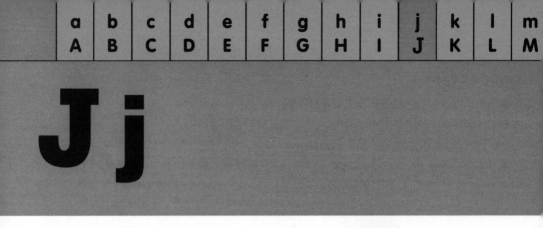

J j

jack-in-the-box / *le diable en boîte*

When you open the lid of a
jack-in-the-box, a funny toy jumps out.

Lorsque tu ouvres le couvercle d'un
***diable en boîte**, un jouet amusant*
en sort.

jar / *le pot*

We can keep sweets in a **jar**.

Nous pouvons ranger des bonbons
*dans un **pot**.*

jeans / *le jean*

Jeans are trousers made from
strong blue cloth.

*Un **jean** est un pantalon de*
tissu bleu très solide.

jelly / *la gelée*

Jelly is a cold, clear, sweet pudding.

*La **gelée** est un dessert froid, clair*
et sucré.

jellyfish / *la méduse*

A **jellyfish** lives in the sea. Jellyfish look as if they are made of jelly.

*La **méduse** vit dans la mer. On dirait que les **méduses** sont faites de gelée.*

jigsaw / *le puzzle*

We have to fit together the pieces of a **jigsaw** puzzle.

*Nous devons mettre ensemble les morceaux d'un **puzzle**.*

juggler / *le jongleur*

A **juggler** throws and catches lots of things all at once.

*Un **jongleur** lance et attrape beaucoup de choses à la fois.*

jumper / *le chandail*

A knitted pullover with long sleeves is a **jumper**.

*Un tricot à longues manches s'appelle un **chandail**.*

K k

kangaroo / *le kangourou*

A **kangaroo** is an Australian animal which carries its baby in a pouch.

*Le **kangourou** est un animal australien qui transporte son bébé dans une poche.*

key / *la clé*

You open a lock with a **key**.

*Tu ouvres une serrure avec une **clé**.*

king / *le roi*

A **king** is the head of a country.

*Le **roi** est le chef d'un pays.*

kiss / *le baiser*

The girl is giving the baby a **kiss**.

*La fille donne un **baiser** au bébé.*

kite / *le cerf-volant*

The boy is flying a **kite**. He must hold on to the string of his **kite**.

*Le garçon fait voler un **cerf-volant**. Il doit tenir la ficelle de son **cerf-volant**.*

kitten / *le chaton*

A **kitten** is a young cat.
*Un **chaton** est un jeune chat.*

knee / *le genou*

Your leg bends in the middle of the **knee**.
*Ta jambe se plie en deux au **genou**.*

knife / *le couteau*

We cut things with a **knife**.
*Nous coupons des choses avec un **couteau**.*

Ll

ladder / l'échelle

You climb a **ladder** to get up to high things.

*Tu montes à **l'échelle** pour atteindre des choses élevées.*

ladybird / *la coccinelle*

A **ladybird** is a red or yellow insect with spots on its back.

*Une **coccinelle** est un insecte rouge ou jaune avec des taches sur le dos.*

lake / *le lac*

A **lake** is a lot of water with land all round it.

*Un **lac** est une grande étendue d'eau entourée de terre.*

lamb / *l'agneau*

A **lamb** is a young sheep.

*Un **agneau** est un jeune mouton.*

lamp / *la lampe*

A **lamp** gives us light. When it gets dark, we switch on the **lamp**.

*Une **lampe** donne de la lumière. Lorsqu'il fait noir, nous allumons la **lampe**.*

leaf / *la feuille*

A **leaf** will grow on a tree or a plant.

*Une **feuille** pousse sur un arbre ou une plante.*

leap-frog / *le saute-mouton*

It is fun to play **leap-frog**.
In **leap-frog**, you leap over your friends' backs.

*C'est amusant de jouer à **saute-mouton**.
Au **saute-mouton**, tu sautes par-dessus le dos de tes amis.*

leg / *la jambe*

We have two **legs**. The boy is waving one **leg** in the air.

*Nous avons deux **jambes**. Le garçon secoue une **jambe** en l'air.*

lemon / *le citron*

A **lemon** is a yellow fruit with a bitter taste.

*Le **citron** est un fruit jaune au goût sur.*

leopard / *le léopard*

A **leopard** is a large, wild animal with a spotted coat.

*Le **léopard** est un grand animal sauvage à fourrure tachetée.*

letter / *la lettre*

When we write a **letter**, we are sending a message to someone.

*Lorsque nous écrivons une **lettre**, nous envoyons un message à quelqu'un.*

library / *la bibliothèque*

A **library** is a room or a building where books are kept.

*Une **bibliothèque** est une pièce ou un bâtiment où l'on range les livres.*

lighthouse / *le phare*

A **lighthouse** is a tall building with a light on top to warn ships of danger.

*Un **phare** est un haut bâtiment avec une lumière au sommet pour prévenir les navires du danger.*

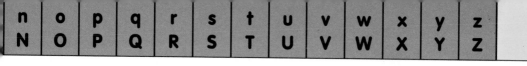

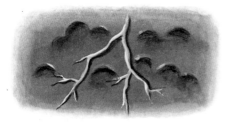

lightning / *l'éclair*

Lightning is the flash that we see in the sky during a thunderstorm.

***L'éclair** est la lumière que nous voyons dans le ciel durant un orage.*

lion / *le lion*

A **lion** is a fierce, wild animal. **Lions** are part of the cat family.

*Un **lion** est un animal sauvage féroce. Les **lions** font partie de la famille des chats.*

lizard / *le lézard*

A **lizard** is an animal with short legs and a long tail.

*Un **lézard** est un animal à courtes pattes et à longue queue.*

lock / *le cadenas*

The cupboard has a **lock** on it. You need a key to un**lock** the cupboard.

*Il y a un **cadenas** sur l'armoire. Tu as besoin d'une clé pour ouvrir l'armoire.*

locomotive / *le locomotive*

The machine that pulls a train is called a **locomotive**.

*La machine qui tire le train s'appelle une **locomotive**.*

lollipop / *la sucette*

A **lollipop** is a sweet on a stick. We lick a **lollipop**.

*Une **sucette** est un bonbon sur un bâton. On suce une **sucette**.*

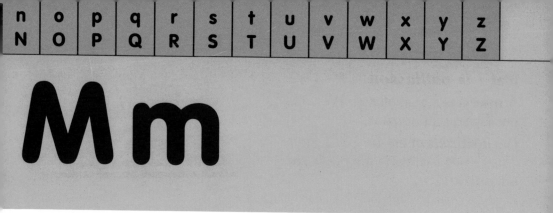

Mm

machine / *la machine*

A **machine** is something that helps us to do work. We clean clothes in a washing-**machine**.

*Une **machine** est quelque chose qui nous aide à faire notre travail. Nous nettoyons les vêtements dans une **machine** à laver.*

magic / *la magie*

The man is doing **magic** tricks. It is difficult to understand how a **magic** trick works.

*L'homme fait des tours de **magie**. Il est difficile de comprendre les tours de **magie**.*

mask / *le masque*

The boy is wearing a **mask**. His face is covered with a **mask**.

*Le garçon porte un **masque**. Il a un **masque** sur le visage.*

mat / *le paillasson*

A **mat** is like a small rug. We wipe our feet on a door**mat**.

*Un **paillasson** est un petit tapis. Nous nous essuyons les pieds sur un **paillasson**.*

medicine / *le médicament*

Medicine is something we take to make us better.

*Un **médicament** est quelque chose que nous prenons pour nous soigner.*

mermaid / *la sirène*

In stories, a **mermaid** is a woman who lives in the sea and has a fish's tail.

*Dans les histoires, une **sirène** est une dame qui vit dans la mer et qui a une queue de poisson.*

milk / *le lait*

Milk is a white drink that comes from cows. Children drink a lot of **milk**.

*Le **lait** est un breuvage blanc qui vient des vaches. Les enfants boivent beaucoup de **lait**.*

mirror / *le miroir*

A **mirror** is a piece of glass that we can see ourselves in.

*Un **miroir** est un morceau de verre dans lequel nous pouvons nous voir.*

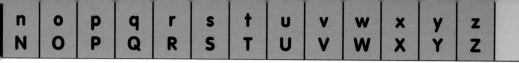

n	o	p	q	r	s	t	u	v	w	x	y	z
N	O	P	Q	R	S	T	U	V	W	X	Y	Z

mole / *la taupe*

A **mole** is a furry animal that lives underground.

*Une **taupe** est un animal à poils qui vit sous la terre.*

moneybox / *la tirelire*

We keep our savings in a **moneybox**.

*Nous gardons nos économies dans une **tirelire**.*

monkey / *le singe*

A **monkey** is a wild, furry animal which is very good at climbing.

*Le **singe** est un animal sauvage à poils qui grimpe très bien.*

mountain / *la montagne*

A hill that is very high is called a **mountain**.

*Une très haute colline s'appelle une **montagne**.*

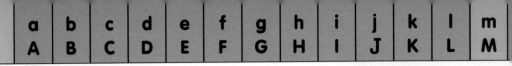

mouse / *la souris*

A **mouse** is a tiny animal with a long tail and sharp teeth.

*Une **souris** est un tout petit animal à longue queue et à dents pointues.*

mouth / *la bouche*

A **mouth** is the opening in our face. We talk and eat with our **mouths**.

*La **bouche** est l'ouverture dans notre visage. Nous parlons et mangeons avec notre **bouche**.*

mushroom / *le champignon*

A **mushroom** is a small plant that grows in woods and fields.

*Un **champignon** est une petite plante qui pousse dans les bois et les champs.*

music / *la musique*

Music is the nice sound you make when you sing. Guitar **music** also sounds good.

*La **musique** est le son agréable que tu fais lorsque tu chantes. La guitare fait aussi de la **musique** agréable.*

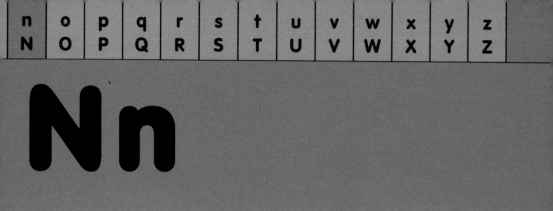

Nn

neck / *le cou*

The **neck** is the part of the body that joins the head to the shoulders. Giraffes have very long **necks**.

*Le **cou** est la partie du corps qui relie la tête aux épaules. Les girafes ont de très longs **cous**.*

necklace / *le collier*

Some people wear a decoration round their neck called a **necklace**.

*Certaines personnes portent une décoration autour du cou que l'on appelle un **collier**.*

needle / *l'aiguille*

We use a **needle** for sewing.

*Nous utilisons une **aiguille** pour coudre.*

nest / *le nid*

Birds, and some other animals, make a home called a **nest**.

*Les oiseaux, et certains autres animaux, fabriquent des maisons que l'on appelle des **nids**.*

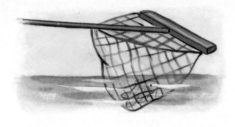

net / *le filet*

Sometimes a **net** is used for catching fish.

*Parfois on utilise un **filet** pour attraper des poissons.*

newt / *la salamandre*

A **newt** is like a lizard that lives partly in water.

*Une **salamandre** est un genre de lézard qui vit en partie dans l'eau.*

nose / *le nez*

We breathe and smell through our **nose**.

*Nous respirons et sentons avec notre **nez**.*

nurse / *l'infirmière*

A **nurse** looks after us when we are sick.

*Une **infirmière** s'occupe de nous lorsque nous sommes malades.*

nuts / *les noix*

When we have taken off the hard shells, we can eat **nuts**.

*Lorsque nous avons enlevé la coquille dure, nous pouvons manger les **noix**.*

Oo

oar / *la rame*

An **oar** is a long piece of wood with one flat end used to move a rowing boat.

*Une **rame** est un long morceau de bois, plat à un bout, utilisée pour faire avancer un bateau à rames.*

ocean / *l'océan*

An **ocean** is a very large sea. One **ocean** is the Atlantic **Ocean**.

*Un **océan** est une très grande mer. Un des **océans** s'appelle l'**océan** Atlantique.*

octopus / *la pieuvre*

An **octopus** lives in the sea.

It has eight long legs with suckers on them.

*Une **pieuvre** vit dans la mer. Elle a huit longs bras couverts de ventouses.*

onion / *l'oignon*

Onions are good to eat. We cry when we cut an **onion**.

*Les **oignons** sont bons à manger. Nous pleurons lorsque nous coupons un **oignon**.*

orange / l'orange

Orange is a colour. The boy's jumper is **orange**.

*L'orange est une couleur. Le chandail du garçon est **orange**.*

orange / l'orange

An **orange** is a kind of fruit. **Oranges** are sweet and good to eat.

*Une **orange** est un sorte de fruit. Les **oranges** sont sucrées et bonnes.*

orchard / le verger

A field full of fruit trees is called an **orchard**.

*Un champ plein d'arbres fruitiers s'appelle un **verger**.*

orchestra / l'orchestre

A lot of people making music together is called an **orchestra**.

*Un groupe de personnes qui jouent de la musique ensemble s'appelle un **orchestre**.*

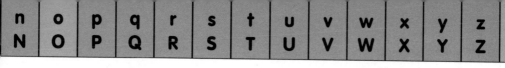

n	o	p	q	r	s	t	u	v	w	x	y	z
N	O	P	Q	R	S	T	U	V	W	X	Y	Z

ostrich / l' autruche

The **ostrich** is the largest bird in the world. An **ostrich** cannot fly.

*L'autruche est le plus gros oiseau au monde. Une **autruche** ne peut pas voler.*

otter / la loutre

An **otter** is a brown, furry animal which swims well and eats fish.

*Une **loutre** est un animal à poils marron qui nage bien et mange du poisson.*

oven / le four

We cook lots of things like cakes and biscuits in an **oven**.

*On cuit beaucoup de choses, comme des gâteaux et des biscuits, au **four**.*

overalls / la combinaison

We wear **overalls** when working, to keep our clothes clean.

*Nous portons une **combinaison** pour travailler, pour ne pas salir nos vêtements.*

owl / le hibou

An **owl** is a bird with a big head and big eyes. **Owls** can see well in the dark.

*Un **hibou** est un oiseau avec une grosse tête et de gros yeux. Les **hibous** voient bien dans le noir.*

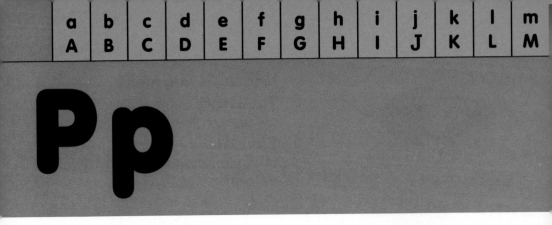

Pp

pail / *le seau*
Jack and Jill carried a **pail** of water.
Jacques et Jeanne ont porté un ***seau*** *d'eau.*

paint / *la peinture*
We put **paint** on things to make them bright and pretty.
Nous mettons de la ***peinture*** *sur les objets pour les colorer et les rendre jolis.*

pancake / *la crêpe*
A **pancake** is flat and round, and good to eat.
Une ***crêpe*** *est plate et ronde, et délicieuse.*

panda / *le panda*
A **panda** is a big, black and white bear.
Un ***panda*** *est un gros ours noir et blanc.*

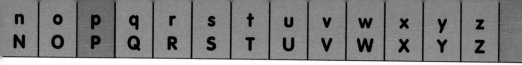

n	o	p	q	r	s	t	u	v	w	x	y	z
N	O	P	Q	R	S	T	U	V	W	X	Y	Z

parade / *le défilé*

It is fun to watch a circus **parade**.

C'est amusant de regarder le **défilé** *d'un cirque.*

park / *le parc*

A **park** is a place with grass and trees, where anyone can play.

Un **parc** *est un endroit avec de l'herbe et des arbres où tout le monde peut jouer.*

parrot / *le perroquet*

A **parrot** is a colourful bird which can learn to say some words.

Un **perroquet** *est un oiseau aux plumes colorées qui peut apprendre à dire quelques mots.*

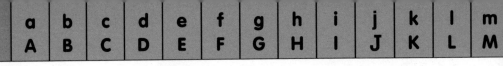

party / *la fête*

At a **party**, we have lots of fun.
We have a **party** on our birthday.

*Durant une **fête**, on s'amuse beaucoup. Nous faisons la **fête** pour notre anniversaire.*

paw / *la patte*

A **paw** is an animal's foot with claws.
Dogs and cats have **paws**.

*Une **patte** est le pied d'un animal muni de griffes. Les chiens et les chats ont des **pattes**.*

peacock / *le paon*

A **peacock** is a bird with a tail of colourful feathers.

*Un **paon** est un oiseau avec une queue au plumage coloré.*

pen / *le crayon* / *le stylo*

We can write and draw with a **pen**.

*Nous pouvons écrire et dessiner avec un **crayon** ou un **stylo**.*

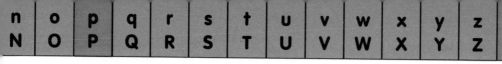

pets / *les animaux de compagnie*

Pets are animals that we keep as special friends. A **pet** can be a dog, a cat, a rabbit, a canary or a goldfish.

*Les **animaux de compagnie** sont nos amis spéciaux. Un **animal de compagnie** peut être un chien, un chat, un lapin, un canari ou un poisson rouge.*

piano / *le piano*

We can make music with a **piano**.

*Nous pouvons jouer de la musique avec un **piano**.*

picnic / *le pique-nique*

When we eat outdoors, we are having a **picnic**.

*Lorsque nous mangeons dehors, nous faisons un **pique-nique**.*

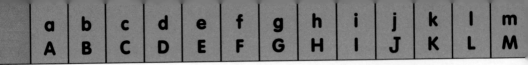

pie / *la tarte*

A **pie** is filled with fruit or meat and cooked in the oven.

*Une **tarte** est garnie de fruits ou de viande et est cuite au four.*

pig / *le cochon*

A **pig** is a pink animal with a curly tail.

*Un **cochon** est un animal rose à la queue en tire-bouchon.*

pigeon / *le pigeon*

A **pigeon** is a bird which can find its way home from far away.

*Un **pigeon** est un oiseau qui peut retrouver le chemin de sa maison de très loin.*

pilot / *le pilote*

A **pilot** is the person who flies an aircraft.

*Le **pilote** est la personne qui **pilote** un avion.*

pink / *le rose*

Pink is a colour. The ballet shoes are **pink**.

*Le **rose** est une couleur. Les chaussons de danse sont **roses**.*

pirate / *le pirate*

A **pirate** is someone who robs from ships.

*Un **pirate** est une personne qui pille les navires.*

pocket / *la poche*

A **pocket** is like a little bag in our clothes where we can keep things.

*Une **poche** est un genre de petit sac dans nos vêtements où nous pouvons mettre des choses.*

polar bear / *l'ours polaire*

A **polar bear** is a wild animal that lives in very cold places.

*Un **ours polaire** est un animal sauvage qui vit dans des endroits très froids.*

pond / *la mare*

A **pond** is a small patch of water. Sometimes we have a **pond** in the garden.

*Une **mare** est une petite étendue d'eau. Parfois nous avons une **mare** dans le jardin.*

a	b	c	d	e	f	g	h	i	j	k	l	m
A	B	C	D	E	F	G	H	I	J	K	L	M

pony / *le poney*
A **pony** is a little horse.
*Un **poney** est un petit cheval.*

puppet / *la marionnette*
We play with a **puppet** by moving its
strings. There are also glove **puppets**.
*Nous jouons avec une **marionnette**
en faisant bouger ses fils. Il y a aussi
des **marionnettes** à gaine.*

puppy / *le chiot*
A **puppy** is a young dog.
*Un **chiot** est un jeune chien.*

purple / *le violet*
Purple is a colour. The flowers
are **purple**.
*Le **violet** est une couleur. Les
fleurs sont **violettes**.*

purse / *le porte-monnaie*
We put money in a **purse** to
keep it safe.
*Nous mettons l'argent dans un
porte-monnaie pour ne pas
le perdre.*

Qq

quack / *le couac*

Ducks **quack**. "**Quack**" is the sound they make.

*Les canards font **couac**. «**Couac**» est le son que font les canards.*

queen / *la reine*

A **queen** is the head of a country. The wife of a king is also a **queen**.

*Une **reine** est le chef d'un pays. La femme d'un roi s'appelle aussi une **reine**.*

quilt / *le duvet*

A **quilt** is the warm, padded cover on our bed.

*Le **duvet** est la couverture chaude et matelassée sur notre lit.*

quiver / *le carquois*

We carry arrows in a **quiver**.

*Nous portons des flèches dans un **carquois**.*

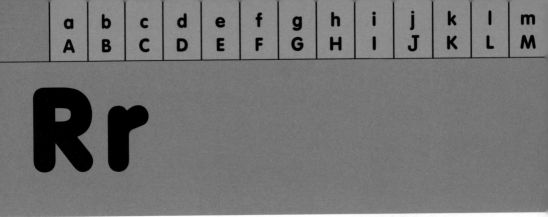

Rr

rabbit / *le lapin*

A **rabbit** is a small, furry animal, with very long ears.

*Un **lapin** est un petit animal à poils, avec de très longues oreilles.*

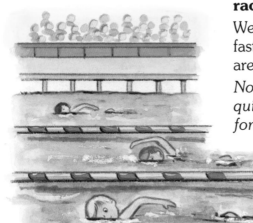

race / *la course*

We have a **race** to see who is the fastest at something. The children are in a swimming **race**.

*Nous faisons la **course** pour voir qui est le plus rapide. Les enfants font une **course** de natation.*

raft / *le radeau*

A **raft** is a flat boat made out of wood.

*Un **radeau** est un bateau plat en bois.*

railway / *le chemin de fer*

A **railway** is the rail track that trains and trams run on.

*Le **chemin de fer** est la voie sur laquelle les trains et les tramways roulent.*

rain / *la pluie*

Rain falls on us from the clouds. We get wet when it is **raining**.

*La **pluie** qui nous tombe dessus vient des nuages. Nous sommes mouillés lorsqu'il **pleut**.*

rainbow / *l'arc-en-ciel*

When the sun shines after it has rained, we sometimes see a **rainbow**.

*Quand le soleil brille après la pluie, nous voyons parfois un **arc-en-ciel**.*

rattle / *le hochet*

A baby will play with a **rattle**. A **rattle** makes a rattling noise.

*Un bébé joue avec un **hochet**. Un **hochet** fait des bruits secs.*

red / *le rouge*

Red is a colour. The bus is **red**.

*Le **rouge** est une couleur.*
*L'autobus est **rouge**.*

reindeer / *le renne*

A **reindeer** is an animal with very large horns.

*Un **renne** est un animal avec de très grands bois.*

ring / *la bague*

Sometimes we wear a **ring** on our finger. A **ring** is a circle.

*Parfois nous portons une **bague** au doigt. Une **bague** est un cercle.*

river / *la rivière*

A **river** is a large stream of moving water.

*Une **rivière** est un gros cours d'eau.*

robot / *le robot*

This toy **robot** is a machine in the shape of a person.

*Ce **robot**-jouet est une machine qui ressemble à une personne.*

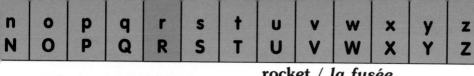

n	o	p	q	r	s	t	u	v	w	x	y	z
N	O	P	Q	R	S	T	U	V	W	X	Y	Z

rocket / *la fusée*

A **rocket** shoots up into the air. It is fun to see **rockets** when they are fireworks.

*Une **fusée** monte en chandelle. Il est amusant de regarder les **fusées** durant les feux d'artifice.*

rocking horse / *le cheval à bascule*

When we are little, we can play on a **rocking horse.**

*Lorsque nous sommes petits, nous pouvons jouer sur un **cheval à bascule.***

roller skates / *les patins à roulettes*

We can move fast when we play on **roller skates**.

*Nous pouvons avancer vite lorsque nous faisons du **patin à roulettes**.*

root / *la racine*

A **root** is the part of a tree or plant under the ground.

*Une **racine** est la partie d'un arbre ou d'une plante qui est sous la terre.*

runway / *la piste*

Aircraft land and take off from a **runway**. A **runway** is a road for aircraft.

*Les avions atterrissent et décollent sur une **piste**. Une **piste** est une route pour avions.*

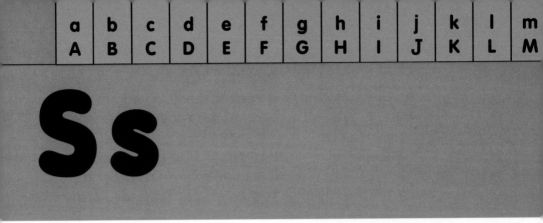

Ss

saddle / *la selle*

You sit in a **saddle** when you ride a horse.

*Tu t'assois sur une **selle** lorsque tu montes à cheval.*

sail / *la voile*

The wind blows into the **sail** and moves the boat along.

*Le vent souffle sur la **voile** et fait avancer le bateau.*

salad / *la salade*

A **salad** is a mixture of vegetables or fruit. **Salads** are cold.

*Une **salade** est un mélange de légumes ou de fruits. Les **salades** sont froides.*

sandcastle / *le château de sable*

It is fun to build a **sandcastle** on the beach.

*C'est amusant de construire un **château de sable** à la plage.*

Santa Claus / *le Père Noël*

Santa Claus brings us presents at Christmas.

*Le **Père Noël** nous amène des cadeaux à Noël.*

sausages / *les saucisses*

Here is a string of **sausages**. Most children enjoy eating **sausages**.

*Voici un chapelet de **saucisses**. La plupart des enfants aiment manger des **saucisses**.*

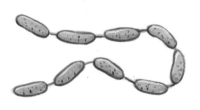

saw / *la scie*

A **saw** has a sharp, jagged edge. We cut things with a **saw**.

*Une **scie** a une lame tranchante et dentée. Nous coupons des choses avec une **scie**.*

school / l'école

People go to **school** to learn things. Children learn to read and write at **school**.

*On va à **l'école** pour apprendre. Les enfants apprennent à lire et à écrire à **l'école**.*

scissors / les ciseaux

Scissors will cut paper and cloth. We say that we have a pair of **scissors.**

*Les **ciseaux** coupent le papier et le tissu. On dit qu'on a une paire de **ciseaux**.*

sea / la mer

The **sea** is the water that covers most of the earth. **Sea** water is salty.

*La **mer** est l'eau qui recouvre presque toute la terre. L'eau de **mer** est salée.*

seal / le phoque

A **seal** is an animal with fur and flippers which spends most of its time in the sea.

*Un **phoque** est un animal à poils et à nageoires qui passe la plupart de son temps dans la mer.*

seashell / *le coquillage*

We find **seashells** beside the sea. A little animal used to live in every **seashell**.

*Nous trouvons des **coquillages** à la plage. Un petit animal habitait dans chaque **coquillage**.*

---

see-saw / *la bascule*

The children are playing on the **see-saw**.

*Les enfants jouent à la **bascule**.*

shadow / *l'ombre*

A light in front of us makes a **shadow** behind us.

*Une lumière devant nous crée une **ombre** derrière nous.*

---

shark / *le requin*

A **shark** lives in the sea. Some **sharks** eat people!

*Le **requin** vit dans la mer. Certains **requins** mangent les gens!*

---

sheep / *le mouton*

We keep **sheep** on farms. Wool is made from a **sheep's** coat.

*On élève les **moutons** à la ferme. La laine provient de la toison du **mouton**.*

ship / *le navire*

We travel across the sea in a **ship**. Some **ships** are very big.

Nous voyageons en mer sur un ***navire***. *Certains* ***navires*** *sont très grands.*

shop / *le magasin*

We can buy things in a **shop**.

Nous pouvons acheter des choses dans un ***magasin***.

shower / *la douche*

A **shower** sprays us with water so that we can wash ourselves.

Une ***douche*** *nous arrose d'eau, pour que nous puissions nous laver.*

signpost / *le panneau*

A **signpost** points the way to somewhere.

Un ***panneau*** *indique comment se rendre quelque part.*

singer / *le chanteur / la chanteuse*

Someone who makes music with their voice is a **singer**.

Quelqu'un qui fait de la musique avec sa voix s'appelle un ***chanteur*** *ou une* ***chanteuse***.

skateboard / *la planche à roulettes*

A **skateboard** is a board with wheels which you can play on.

*Une **planche à roulettes** est une planche munie de roulettes sur laquelle tu peux jouer.*

skeleton / *le squelette*

Our **skeleton** is made up of all the bones in our body.

*Notre **squelette** est fait de tous les os de notre corps.*

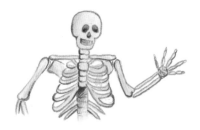

sleep / *dormir*

We go to bed to **sleep**. When we are tired, we need to have a **sleep**.

*Nous allons au lit pour **dormir**. Quand nous sommes fatigués, nous avons besoin de **dormir**.*

sleigh / *le traîneau*

We travel over the snow in a **sleigh**. Santa uses a **sleigh**.

*Nous voyageons sur la neige en **traîneau**. Le Père Noël utilise un **traîneau**.*

smoke / *la fumée*

Smoke is the dark cloud that we see when something is burning.

*La **fumée** est le nuage sombre que nous voyons lorsque quelque chose brûle.*

snail / *l'escargot*

A **snail** is a small animal with a shell on its back which moves very slowly.

*Un **escargot** est un petit animal qui a une coquille sur le dos et qui se déplace très lentement.*

snakes / *les serpents*

Snakes are long, thin animals without legs. A **snake** slides along the ground.

*Les **serpents** sont des animaux longs et minces sans pattes. Un **serpent** se déplace en glissant par terre.*

snow / *la neige*

When it is cold, flakes of frozen water called **snow** fall from the sky.

*Quand il fait froid, des flocons d'eau gelée, que l'on appelle **neige**, tombent du ciel.*

spider / *l'araignée*

A **spider** is a small animal with eight legs which makes a web to catch its food.

*Une **araignée** est un petit animal à huit pattes qui tisse des toiles pour attraper à manger.*

squirrel / *l'écureuil*

A **squirrel** is a red or grey animal with a bushy tail. **Squirrels** live in trees.

*Un **écureuil** est un animal roux ou gris à queue touffue. Les **écureuils** vivent dans les arbres.*

stars / *les étoiles*

We see tiny lights in the sky at night. They are the **stars**.

*Nous voyons de toutes petites lumières dans le ciel la nuit. Ce sont les **étoiles**.*

starfish / *l'étoile de mer*

A **starfish** is a star-shaped fish.

*Une **étoile de mer** est un poisson en forme d'étoile.*

steeple / *le clocher*

A **steeple** is the high, pointed top of a church.

*Le **clocher** est le sommet pointu d'une église.*

storm / *la tempête*

It is a **storm** when there are strong winds and heavy rain.

*Il y a une **tempête** quand le vent souffle fort et qu'il pleut très fort.*

street / *la rue*

A road with houses or shops along it is a **street**.

*Une route longée de maisons ou de magasins s'appelle une **rue**.*

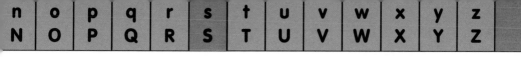

submarine / *le sous-marin*

A **submarine** is a boat that can go under the water.

*Un **sous-marin** est un bateau qui peut aller sous l'eau.*

sunflower / *le tournesol*

A **sunflower** is a large, golden flower which always faces the sun.

*Un **tournesol** est une grosse fleur dorée qui se tourne toujours vers le soleil.*

supermarket / *le supermarché*

A very big shop is called a **supermarket**.

*Un très grand magasin s'appelle un **supermarché**.*

swan / *le cygne*

A **swan** is a big, white bird with a very long neck.

*Un **cygne** est un grand oiseau blanc avec un très long cou.*

Tt

tail / *la queue*

A **tail** is the end of something. Most animals have **tails**.

*La **queue** est la fin de quelque chose. La plupart des animaux ont une **queue**.*

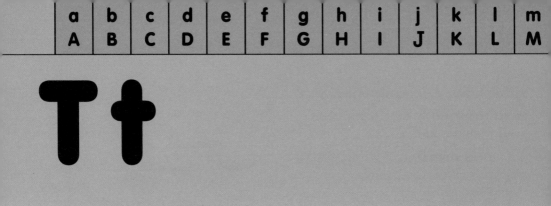

tambourine / *le tambourin*

Sometimes we make music with a **tambourine**.

*Quelque fois nous jouons de la musique avec un **tambourin**.*

tangle / *emmêler*

The dogs' leads are in a **tangle**. They are all knotted together.

*Les laisses des chiens sont **emmêlées**. Elles sont tout embrouillées.*

taxi / *le taxi*

A **taxi** is like a car that will take us places for money.

*Un **taxi** est une voiture qui nous emmènera quelque part pour de l'argent.*

teacher / *le maître d'école* /
la maîtresse d'école

The **teacher** teaches us things at
school.

*La **maîtresse d'école** nous
apprend des choses à l'école.*

Teddy bear / *l'ours en peluche*

A **Teddy bear** is soft and warm.

*Un **ours en peluche** est doux et
chaud.*

telephone / *le téléphone*

We talk on the **telephone** to
someone far away.

*Nous parlons au **téléphone** à
quelqu'un qui est loin.*

television / *la télévision*

Television shows us pictures in our
homes from far away.

*La **télévision** nous montre chez
nous des images de très loin.*

tent / *la tente*

When we are camping, we sleep in a **tent**.

*Quand nous campons, nous dormons sous une **tente**.*

theatre / *le théâtre*

We go to the **theatre** to see actors and hear music.

*Nous allons au **théâtre** pour regarder des acteurs et écouter de la musique.*

thermometer / *le thermomètre*

*When we are not well, a **thermometer** measures how hot we are.*

*Quand nous ne sommes pas bien, un **thermomètre** mesure notre température.*

thumb / *le pouce*

On each hand, we have a **thumb** and four other fingers.

*A chaque main, nous avons un **pouce** et quatre autres doigts.*

tiger / *le tigre*

A **tiger** is a big, wild animal with a striped coat.

*Un **tigre** est un grand animal sauvage à la fourrure rayée.*

toes / *les orteils*

We have five **toes** on the end of each foot.

*Nous avons cinq **orteils** au bout de chaque pied.*

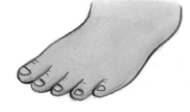

tomato / *la tomate*

A **tomato** is a soft red fruit. We eat **tomatoes** raw or cooked.

*La **tomate** est un fruit rouge et mou. Nous mangeons les **tomates** crues ou cuites.*

tools / *les outils*

Tools help us to do work. A screwdriver is a **tool**.

*Les **outils** nous aident à faire notre travail. Un tournevis est un **outil**.*

tooth / *la dent*

A **tooth** is one of the hard white bones in our mouth. We bite things with our **teeth**.

*Une **dent** est un des os blancs et durs dans notre bouche. Nous mordons les choses avec nos **dents**.*

tortoise / *la tortue*

A **tortoise** is a slow-moving animal with a hard shell on its back.

*Une **tortue** est un animal lent avec une carapace sur le dos.*

tower / *la tour*

The walls of a castle have **towers** at each corner. A **tower** is a tall, narrow building.

*Les murs d'un château ont des **tours** à chaque coin. Une **tour** est un bâtiment haut et étroit.*

toys / *les jouets*

Toy boats and **toy** drums are **toys**.

*Les bateaux miniatures et les tambours d'enfant sont des **jouets**.*

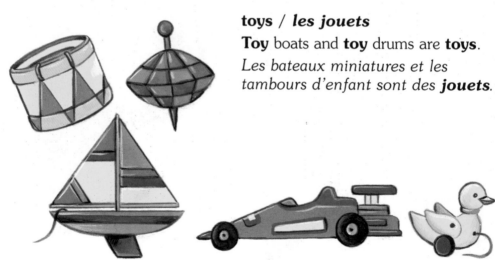

tractor / *le tracteur*

A **tractor** can pull heavy things over muddy ground.

*Un **tracteur** peut tirer des choses lourdes en terrain boueux.*

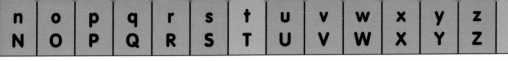

train / *le train*

A **train** is pulled by a locomotive. Sometimes there are lots of wagons in a **train**.

*Un **train** est tiré par une locomotive. Quelquefois un **train** a beaucoup de wagons*

tree / *l'arbre*

A **tree** is a very big plant. **Trees** have branches and leaves.

*Un **arbre** est une très grande plante. Les **arbres** ont des branches et des feuilles.*

truck / *le camion*

Lots of things are carried by road in a **truck**.

*Beaucoup de choses sont transportées en **camion** par la route.*

trumpet / *la trompette*

We can make music by blowing a **trumpet**.

*On peut faire de la musique en soufflant dans une **trompette**.*

tunnel / *le tunnel*

A **tunnel** is a passage under the ground.

*Un **tunnel** est un passage sous terre.*

a	b	c	d	e	f	g	h	i	j	k	l	m
A	B	C	D	E	F	G	H	I	J	K	L	M

Uu

umbrella / *le parapluie*

An **umbrella** will keep us dry when it rains.

*Un **parapluie** nous gardera au sec quand il pleut.*

unicorn / *la licorne*

In fairy tales, a **unicorn** is a magic animal with one horn on its head.

*Dans les contes de fées, une **licorne** est un animal magique avec une corne sur la tête.*

uniform / *l'uniforme*

A **uniform** is a set of special clothes that some people wear. A nurse wears a **uniform**.

*Un **uniforme** est un ensemble de vêtements spéciaux que certaines personnes portent. Une infirmière porte un **uniforme**.*

Vv

vacuum cleaner / *l'aspirateur*
A **vacuum cleaner** is a machine that sucks up dirt.
*Un **aspirateur** est une machine qui aspire la saleté.*

valley / *la vallée*
A **valley** is the low piece of land between hills.
*Une **vallée** est la partie basse entre les collines.*

van / *la camionnette*
A small truck for delivering things is called a **van**.
*Un petit camion de livraison s'appelle une **camionnette**.*

vase / *le vase*
We put flowers in a **vase**.
*Nous mettons des fleurs dans un **vase**.*

vegetables / *les légumes*

Vegetables are plants that we grow for food. **Vegetables** are good for us.

*Les **légumes** sont des plantes que nous faisons pousser pour nous nourrir. Les **légumes** sont bons pour la santé.*

violin / *le violon*

We can make music on a **violin** by rubbing the bow against the strings.

*Nous pouvons jouer de la musique au **violon** en frottant l'archet sur les cordes.*

voice / *la voix*

When we sing and speak, we are using our **voice**.

*Lorsque nous chantons et parlons, nous utilisons notre **voix**.*

W w

wagon / *le wagon*

A **wagon** is a cart for carrying heavy loads. Sometimes a **wagon** is pulled by horses.

*Un **wagon** est un chariot utilisé pour transporter des choses lourdes. Quelquefois un **wagon** est tiré par des chevaux.*

waist / *la taille*

Our **waist** is in the middle of our body. Our body bends at the **waist**.

*Notre **taille** se trouve au milieu de notre corps. Notre corps se plie à la **taille**.*

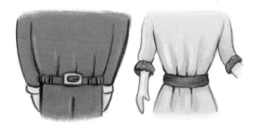

walrus / *le morse*

A **walrus** is a big sea animal with two long tusks.

*Un **morse** est un grand animal de mer avec deux longues défenses.*

watch / *la montre*

A **watch** is like a small clock that we wear on our arm.

*Une **montre** ressemble à une petite horloge que nous portons au bras.*

waterfall / *la cascade*

A stream of water falling over a cliff is called a **waterfall**.

*Un cours d'eau qui tombe d'une falaise s'appelle une **cascade**.*

well / *le puits*

A **well** is a deep hole in the ground with water in it.

*Un **puits** est un trou profond dans la terre avec de l'eau au fond.*

whale / *la baleine*

A **whale** is a big animal that lives in the sea.

*Une **baleine** est un gros animal qui vit dans la mer.*

wheelbarrow / *la brouette*

We use a **wheelbarrow** in the garden. A **wheelbarrow** has two handles and one wheel.

*Nous utilisons une **brouette** dans le jardin. Une **brouette** a deux manches et une roue.*

wigwam / *le wigwam*

A **wigwam** is a kind of tent that some American Indians used to live in.

*Un **wigwam** est un genre de tente dans laquelle certains Amérindiens habitaient.*

windmill / *le moulin à vent*

The wind blows round the sails of the **windmill**. **Windmills** are machines that can lift water.

*Le vent fait tourner les ailes du **moulin à vent**. Les **moulins à vent** sont des machines qui peuvent puiser de l'eau.*

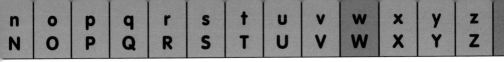

wing / *l'aile*

The **wing** is the part of a bird that it uses to fly. Birds have two **wings**.

*L'**aile** est la partie que l'oiseau utilise pour voler. Les oiseaux ont deux **ailes**.*

woodpecker / *le pivert*

A **woodpecker** is a bird that pecks wood. You can often hear a **woodpecker** tapping on a tree.

*Un **pivert** est un oiseau qui frappe sur le bois. Tu peux souvent entendre un **pivert** frapper sur un arbre.*

a	b	c	d	e	f	g	h	i	j	k	l	m
A	B	C	D	E	F	G	H	I	J	K	L	M

worm / *le ver*

A **worm** is like a little snake that lives in the earth.

*Un **ver** ressemble à un petit serpent qui vit sous terre.*

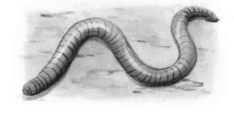

wrist / *le poignet*

Our **wrist** joins our hand to our arm. We have two **wrists**.

*Notre **poignet** relie notre main à notre bras. Nous avons deux **poignets**.*

Xx

X-ray / *les rayons x*

A picture of the inside of our body is called an **x-ray**.

*L'image de l'intérieur de notre corps s'appelle une radio à **rayons x**.*

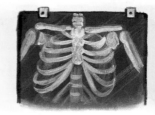

xylophone / *le xylophone*

We play a **xylophone** to make music.

*Nous jouons au **xylophone** pour faire de la musique.*

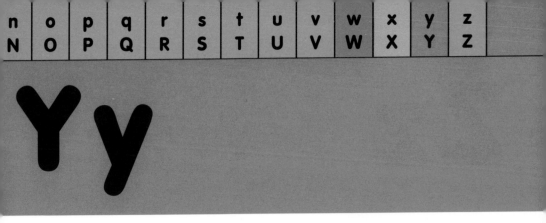

Yy

yacht / *le yacht*
A boat with large sails is called a **yacht**.

*Un bateau à grandes voiles s'appelle un **yacht**.*

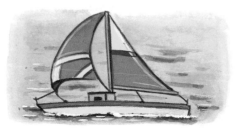

yawn / *bailler*
We **yawn** when we are tired.

*Nous **baillons** quand nous sommes fatigués.*

yellow / *le jaune*
Yellow is a colour. The little bird is **yellow**.

*Le **jaune** est une couleur.*
*Le petit oiseau est **jaune**.*

yo-yo / *le yo-yo*
A **yo-yo** is a toy. We spin a **yo-yo** up and down.

*Un **yo-yo** est un jouet. Nous faisons monter et descendre un **yo-yo**.*

a	b	c	d	e	f	g	h	i	j	k	l	m
A	B	C	D	E	F	G	H	I	J	K	L	M

n	o	p	q	r	s	t
N	O	P	Q	R	S	T

u	v	w	x	y	z
U	V	W	X	Y	Z

Zz

zebra / *le zèbre*

A **zebra** is a wild animal like a striped horse.

*Un **zèbre** est un animal sauvage qui ressemble à un cheval rayé.*

zip / *la fermeture éclair*

A **zip** at the front of our jacket fastens the sides together.

*Une **fermeture éclair** sur le devant de notre veste attache les côtés ensemble.*

This edition first published 2000
Reprinted 2001, 2002
Brown Watson, The Old Mill,
76 Fleckney Road, Kibworth Beauchamp,
Leicestershire, LE8 OHG

©2000 Brown Watson
Printed in the E.C.
ISBN: 0-7097-1379-7